D1325979

Ann Summers

guide to having the

Best Sex Ever

EBURY
PRESS

1 3 5 7 9 10 8 6 4 2

Published in 2009 by Ebury Press, an imprint of Ebury Publishing

A Random House Group Company

Text written by Siobhan Kelly copyright © Ebury Press 2009
Photographs copyright © John Freeman 2009

The Random House Group Limited Reg. No. 954009

Addresses for companies within the Random House Group can be found at
www.randomhouse.co.uk

A CIP catalogue record for this book is available from the British Library

Art direction and design by seagulls.net
Photography by John Freeman

The Random House Group Limited supports The Forest Stewardship Council (FSC),
the leading international forest certification organisation. All our titles that are
printed on Greenpeace approved FSC certified paper carry the FSC logo. Our paper
procurement policy can be found at www.rbooks.co.uk/environment

To buy books by your favourite authors
and register for offers visit www.rbooks.co.uk

Printed and bound in Singapore by Tien Wah Press

ISBN 9780091928230

Contents

Foreword

There is sex. There is good sex. There is great sex.
And then there's the best sex ever – the kind of orgasmic
love-making that you remember for the rest of your life
with a smile on your face and a tingle between your
legs. And this book is about showing you how to have
best-ever sex, every night of the year.

Whether you're a singleton or coupled-up, new to sex
or an old hand, this book is about making sex more
intense, more fun, more enjoyable and more orgasmic.
As well as the usual tips, toys and positions you'd expect
from Ann Summers, we've also persuaded real people
to share the delicious details of the best sex they've ever
had – sizzling stories that will arouse and inspire.

We really hope that you enjoy this book – and that it
helps you take your sex life to the next level!

Jacqueline Gold

Best...
Foreplay
...Ever

Best Mental Foreplay Ever

The largest sexual organ isn't between your legs – it's between your ears. You don't even have to be in the same room to start the mental process of sexual arousal. Get each other thinking about sex long before you touch, and your orgasm will have all day to build and bubble.

Mental foreplay is a particularly good idea if you're in the mood for quickie sex – the more sexually charged you are by the time you meet, the deeper into the stages of psychogenic (non-contact)

arousal you'll be by the time you meet in the flesh – which means virtually zero physical foreplay is needed.

Call your partner and describe in detail the things you'd like to do to them at the end of the day. If you like the idea of talking dirty but the phone makes you tongue-tied, take advantage of text or email. Or why not visit a good erotic fiction website, pick a story that turns you on and suggest re-enacting it.

Alter your environment to suggest sex. Why say 'I want sex' when a candlelit bath strewn with rose petals, or a riding crop laid out on a scarlet silken bedspread speak louder than words ever could?

BEST TIPS EVER

Research from the US suggests that loud, thumping music actually gets your heart rate up and your blood pumping, mimicking sexual arousal. So turn up the bass, turn up the volume, and turn yourselves on.

Striptease blurs the line between mental and physical foreplay – you're putting on a show for your lover, but you're still not allowed to touch.

Here's how to perfect the art of erotic undressing:

Plan carefully. The more you're wearing, the more you can take off. Take your time – the more buttons, zips and belts, the slower it will be.

Think about practicalities. Girls, are you going to keep your suspenders on when you have sex? If so, panties go over the

top. Guys, take your socks off before your trousers. A grown man naked but for socks is not an erotic incentive.

Work to your best features. If you (or your partner) love your top half, make it the first thing you expose. If your legs are amazing, unveil them first and strike some poses which flatter your assets – and your ass.

Caress yourself. Linger over the erogenous zones you'd like him/her to touch later. Always leave your genitals until last. Imagining what's under those panties or boxers is part of the thrill.

Make every kiss count

In an Ann Summers survey, a good old-fashioned kiss came in at number one on a list of top turn-ons. And yet it's one of the first things to fall by the wayside in long-term relationships, with a good, passionate kiss becoming something that's only offered as a prelude to sex. Kissing is to women what oral sex is to men – the one thing we crave but don't get enough of.

Tantric sex says a woman's lower lip is directly linked to her clitoris. Try taking her lower lip lightly between your teeth and sucking gently.

Vary the tempo and the technique. If you usually play tonsil hockey, try kissing without tongues, but with open mouths. A little restraint can encourage you to explore each other's mouths in new ways.

⭐ BEST TIPS EVER
Vow to snog like teenagers for five minutes a day without full sex being on the agenda.

Make your mouth a nice place to hang out. Floss and brush your teeth and tongue to ensure fresh breath. And smile!

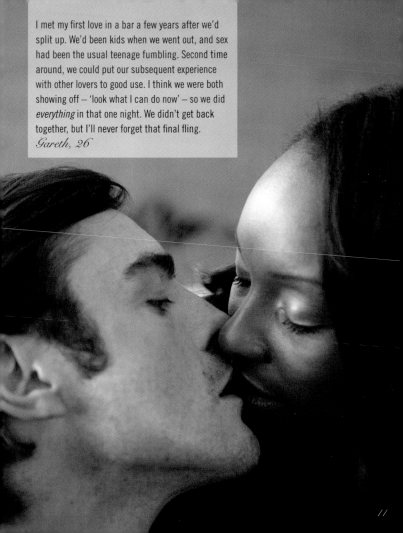

I met my first love in a bar a few years after we'd split up. We'd been kids when we went out, and sex had been the usual teenage fumbling. Second time around, we could put our subsequent experience with other lovers to good use. I think we were both showing off — 'look what I can do now' — so we did *everything* in that one night. We didn't get back together, but I'll never forget that final fling.

Gareth, 26

Best physical foreplay
– how to touch your lover

Sometimes, you're so hot for each other that you can go straight to intercourse with barely a kiss. But most of the time foreplay is the key difference between good and great sex.

Most women say they don't get enough of foreplay. It takes women an average of 20 minutes from arousal to orgasm, during which time she needs to become aroused and lubricated, ready for his penis. It takes men three minutes. Make a vow to fill those 17 minutes with all the kisses and caresses you can give and receive.

We all want to be touched in different ways. Some people like a vigorous massage resembling something you'd get from a sports therapist, others love sexy scratching, while many prefer such a featherlight touch you can barely feel it. There's only one way to find out what your partner's into. Ask for constant feedback – do you like this? What about this? If you're unsure about sex talk, use the moan-o-meter system to rate your touch – loud means good, quiet means less so.

Where's the hand going to go next? Don't use the same touches every time. You'll learn to 'expect' the same touches and won't get so excited. Use wavy lines and trace sweeping patterns on skin rather than straight, smooth strokes – it keeps your partner guessing. Follow your hands with

★ BEST TIPS EVER

If you swirl around her nipple, skimming it but never quite touching it, it'll become erect and sensitive as it craves attention. Whether you choose to lavish it with a kiss now or defer the gratification is up to you…

a trail of little kisses, further tantalising skin that's already tingling with pleasure.

Place a little massage oil between your palms, rub your hands together to warm it up and swirl large, sweeping figure 8s on your lover's body. Body parts particularly receptive to this stylish massage are breasts and butt.

Washing each other's hair is a form of foreplay that dates back to ancient India – the word 'shampoo' actually describes an intimate head massage in the Kama Sutra. Climb into the bathtub together and massage luxurious shampoo into each other's hair, swirling your fingers around and paying particular attention to the hairline and the nape of the neck. Rinse, then comb through conditioner and then tenderly dry each other off. The head is not the most obvious erogenous zone, which is why we often neglect it. Pay it extra attention and you'll be rewarded with a blissed-out feeling that leaves you wanting more.

⭐ BEST TIPS EVER

Touch each other all the time, even when you don't want sex. Thinking of foreplay as an exquisite treat in its own right has two advantages – it takes the pressure off when it comes to intercourse, and it means both your bodies are constantly alive to the possibility of sex.

The more you keep your touch away from the genitals, the more arousing it can be. Tease by skimming the important areas and focus on less obvious hotspots such as knees, inner elbows, armpits and necks. It can be tempting to dive straight for the breasts or genitals, but the longer you leave these most highly erogenous zones, the more delicious tension builds.

Skin-on-skin is an amazing feeling, but why stop there? Caress your lover with

your breath, or a feather, or an ice cube, or a vibrator on a low setting. Try wearing nothing but a pair of black leather gloves next time you massage her. It's a visual kink that conjures up images of fetish clubs and power, as well as being a weird, wonderful feeling.

Use your hands to guide your lover where you want. Just take his hands in yours and lead him to the spot that's begging for his touch. Use your own hand to show him the strokes and rhythm you like, and when he understands, take your own hand away and enjoy the fabulous feeling of being touched just where you want, just how you want it.

Sometimes you need to come right out and tell your partner what you want. Before you do this, say it out loud to yourself first, and imagine how you'd feel if you were on the receiving end of the words. We're all vulnerable to criticism when it comes to sex, and keeping your voice soft and sensitive and choosing your words wisely can make the difference between an upset, offended lover and one who's only too eager to do whatever it takes to get you off.

Prolong the pleasure – don't forget the afterplay. Hold each other, indulge in a little pillow talk and keep the caresses going long after the tingle of orgasm has subsided.

Foreplay for one

The thing about sex is that there doesn't have to be two of you in the room to do it. We're so hung up on penetration that we've lost sight of how important masturbation is. Being able to make yourself come is hugely empowering. After all, how will you ever have great sex with someone else if you don't know what your body needs? As a wise man once said, masturbation is sex with someone you love. So love yourself... all over.

For girls

If you've never masturbated before, don't put any pressure on yourself. Choose a time when your phone's turned off, and you won't be disturbed. Simply caress and stroke yourself down there. If you don't climax, what's the rush? You literally have forever. You're not trying to please a partner. Just yourself.

Fantasise to get your juices flowing – whether that means closing your eyes and thinking about a colleague or ex, or reading an erotic novel, or watching hardcore porn.

Give yourself a little foreplay – touch your breasts and other erogenous zones before you fiddle with your clit. Watch your nipples respond to your own touch. Notice whether your breathing changes as you become aroused. If your clit is begging for your fingers, start by stroking yourself through your knickers.

Positions

The most common one is sitting or lying back, legs spread out. There's a theory that pressing the soles of your feet together makes you more likely to orgasm. Another more animalistic one is crouched on all fours, one hand slipped between your legs or even standing up.

Make your fingers into a V shape at the top of your labia so that the bud of your clitoris is exposed. Start with soft, gentle strokes, all around your clit as well as on it. Some research shows that the skin around the sides of the clit is sensitive in different patches. Try either side and see if that's true for you. Circle and lightly flick it. Keep up a steady rhythm, and see what techniques work for you.

In the power shower, direct a jet of water over your clit and let the current massage you to orgasm. But *don't ever* insert a jet of water into your vagina as it can tear the fine, delicate skin there.

If you usually masturbate with your fingers, try slipping a dildo inside you. Your pussy walls contract when you come, and the difference when there's actually something inside you is stimulating.

The clitoris is the only organ in the human body which exists just for pleasure.

Vibrators are a great way to learn how to orgasm. Set it low at first, and literally sit back and let it happen (*see page 84 to find out which kind of vibrator is right for you*). There's a theory that you can get dependent on sex toys, and there could be some truth in that. Make sure you save the vibrator for an occasional treat.

★ BEST TIPS EVER

When you're on your way to coming, try a Tantric sex trick. Breathe deeply, and instead of picturing your spunk shooting out of your dick, visualise it travelling back up your hard-on and the energy dispersing through your body. This could lead you to a 'dry orgasm', which practitioners say can leave you tingling for hours afterwards.

For boys

Boys are less likely to be told how to masturbate – from the first day they discover it, they have a love affair with their own hand that's the most enduring of all. But did you know you can use your me-time to make yourself an even better lover, and to get more out of sex? Here's how.

If you've never tried commercial lube, give it a go. You'll be amazed how much smoother your touch is.

Pull the skin down your penis, away from your foreskin and towards the base. Twist the skin at the base of your dick. This is an intense high, a sort of mini Chinese burn that you'd never entrust anyone else to do but because it's you, you can experiment with how far you can take this.

Fill a ribbed condom with thick silicone lube and delve into your new, slippery slidey 'tunnel'. If you always use porn, try to get off using just your imagination. Yes, it's a hard habit to break, but it'll take you longer to come and your orgasm will be that much stronger because of the deferred gratification.

Don't rush to the finish line. Men often come in two seconds flat – because masturbation time is often snatched – but by slowing down your breathing and concentrating hard, you can actually delay your orgasm time. As you feel yourself approach climax, but before it's too late, stop touching yourself until you lose your hard-on. Then start again, then stop again. With practice, you should be able to hold out for up to five times as long. The explosion, when it comes, will be worth the wait.

The average time a man can keep an erection is 40 minutes.

Best...
Hand-jobs
...Ever

Want to be a red-hot lover and have red-hot sex? Then you'd better be good with your hands. Intimate touch is a skill that lovers of either sex can learn with just a few easy-to-learn, fun-to-practise techniques.

Lubrication, lubrication, lubrication!

When she becomes aroused, a woman's natural juices automatically make penetration easier. But sometimes you want to go on playing for longer than her natural lubrication lasts. Experimentation is the key to having your best-ever sex, and lube frees you up to experiment into infinity. A slick of lube can make the difference between abandoning a sex position or masturbation technique because she's dry and sore, and being able to keep going until she sees stars. And, of course, the anus doesn't make any natural lubrication at all, so it's vital to use lube when having anal sex. The question is which type to use.

Water-based lubes like KY jelly are non sticky and don't stain. If you're ever in doubt, opt for water-based.

pussy rub

warms, intensifies and heightens orgasms

Ann Summers

However, they can dry out, so you might have to re-apply them.

Oil-based lubricants last longer and feel nice and slippery, but can break down condoms within 60 seconds. They're not easy to wash off and can ruin sex toys.

Silicone lubes represent the cutting edge and last for as long as you can keep going (they're actually based on the lubricant NASA uses keep its spaceships moving smoothly). They shouldn't break down condoms and are thick – great for anal play.

Flavoured and perfumed lubes can really enhance oral sex. They're designed to be used all over the body, licked off nipples and massaged into inner thighs, as well as for penetrative use. Not all of them are suitable for internal use, or latex compatible, so check the label first.

Self-heating lubes contain ingredients that bring about a warm, tingly feeling when they come into contact with water, saliva or natural juices. They can be pretty powerful, so experiment with tiny amounts first.

Go easy with petroleum jelly, hair conditioner, sun lotion, or cooking fat. Many of them contain harsh chemicals, and they can also break down the rubber in condoms.

For her

Many women just can't orgasm through intercourse alone – they need clitoral stimulation, too. Luckily, that's easily done...

The most common position for masturbating a woman is to kneel or lie between her legs. This is fabulous if you want to alternate fingers and tongues and move into oral sex. Rest your wrist and forearm on her pubic bone – you could be here a while, and you don't want tiredness to interrupt your steady rhythm (*see page 28*). Other fun positions include lying side by side in bed, or behind her then reaching in between her legs. These are both great for kissing and nuzzling her neck if that's what turns her on. Use a little lube for a smooth ride. Women can be highly aroused without getting very wet – anything from dehydration to anti-histamine medication can interfere with her ability to lubricate, so a little commercial lube on hand means you'll never run out of juice – and you can go on for as long as it takes.

Ask her to help you out – if she makes an upside-down 'V' shape with her two forefingers and stretches back the skin either side of her clit, it's exposed and sensitive and ready for your touch.

Don't touch the clitoris itself right away. The nerve endings bundled up in this little bud of flesh actually fan out for several centimetres either side of her clitoris, through her labia and

⭐ BEST TIPS EVER

Research suggests that some women can orgasm more easily when the skin to one side of the clitoris is stimulated than by direct clit stimulation itself. Experiment with this, using the tip of your finger, or the tip of your penis, to nuzzle away at the skin all around her clitoris and search for her secret hotspot.

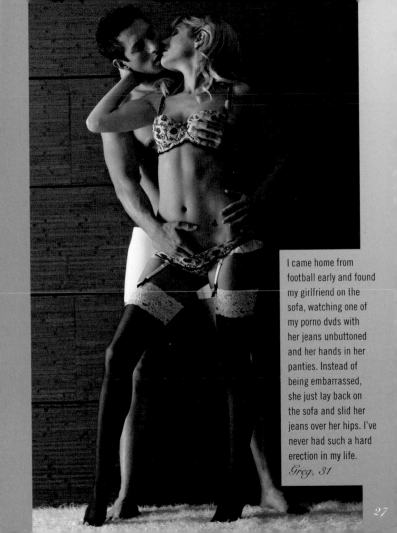

I came home from football early and found my girlfriend on the sofa, watching one of my porno dvds with her jeans unbuttoned and her hands in her panties. Instead of being embarrassed, she just lay back on the sofa and slid her jeans over her hips. I've never had such a hard erection in my life.

Greg, 31

into her whole pelvis. Use your two forefingers to slide either side down the clit, closing them slightly as you slide over it. Trail your fingers over her labia, and repeat the process.

10% of women orgasm in their sleep.

Most women prefer you to start softly and gradually increase the pressure and pace until you find one she's happy with. Start with soft, subtle strokes and tell her she can keep shouting 'more' until you find a stroke that's right for her. Once you've hit on a rhythm she likes, keep it consistent. Men tend to want firmer and faster pressure as they hurtle towards orgasm, but for women consistency is key.

It can be a huge visual treat for you to slide your fingers in and out of her pussy but don't do this if it means neglecting the clitoris. The key here is clit stimulation, not penetration. That said, if you know she's approaching orgasm, a couple of fingers inside her will give her pussy walls something to hug onto when she convulses with pleasure.

The typical female orgasm lasts six to ten seconds but the longest ever was 20 (now that's what I call a best ever!)

To locate and stimulate her G-spot, get behind her when she's on all fours. Make sure she's already aroused – you can't find the G-spot unless she's turned on, so do whatever it takes to get her horny. Slide a warm, well-lubed finger inside her and 'beckon' towards the front of her pussy. Can you feel a little bean-shaped nodule about halfway up? Gently stroke and press it and see what happens.

For him

Many women are nervous about giving hand-jobs, and understandably so. After all, he's been practising his whole life! But a little knowledge goes a long way...

To give him the best-ever hand-job, do something he can't – kneel between his legs and approach his dick from underneath. Make eye contact with him but don't forget to cast admiring glances at what lies in his lap, too. Gently flutter your hands up and down the shaft of his penis before progressing to the more firm, rhythmic strokes.

Use lube. Some men use it when they masturbate, as without it the friction of palm on penis can cross the wrong side of the pleasure/pain line! Warm it between your palms first.

Make a loose fist with one hand and slide it all the way up the shaft of the penis, and this next bit is the key – twist it with a little flourish at the top. This little flick pays attention to the head of his penis and the top few centimetres, which are by far the most sensitive parts. Keep moving – when one hand gets to the top, the other's at the bottom, ready to start stroking again. Pay attention to his balls. Stroke the line that divides them with the tip of your thumb and cup them gently in your palm. For some men this is seventh heaven, for others it's hell, so don't take it personally if he doesn't like it. If he does, then he's a ballboy – progress to the next tip!

Press your thumb and forefingers together, as though you were trying to make a beak. Clasp his testicles gently between the beak-like shape formed by your fingers. Using a gentle circular motion, give them a little pull. Next, relax your fingertips and swirl them up his penis and back down. Repeat as an upward movement starting at the base.

Circumcised men vary tremendously. Some have much less sensitivity requiring more stimulation, while others retain their sensitivity. The only way to find out what the willy you're with wants is to ask!

⭐ BEST TIPS EVER

Press firmly on his perineum – the hairless patch between his balls and bum – to stimulate his prostate gland, also known as the 'male G-spot'. This sensitive area can trip him over the edge into an extra-powerful, best-ever orgasm.

Best...
Oral Sex
...Ever

More, more, more! Men and women both report that they don't get enough oral sex. Following these steps means even a novice can give best-ever oral sex and you'll never need to go without this delicious treat again.

The best blow-job ever!

There's an old joke that says there's no such thing as a bad blow-job. Maybe. But why settle for 'not bad' when 'best-ever' is an option? It is, after all, the one treat he'll never be able to lavish upon himself...

The best positions for fellatio? She kneels on all fours while he lies prostate on his back, or he stands while she kneels at his feet. The first one gives her a little more power and control; the second one makes the guy feel hugely empowered and masculine. Another favourite position involves the woman lying back while he crouches over her, but be warned, as she can't control the angle at which he penetrates her mouth, she may find that she gags on his penis.

> ⭐ BEST TIPS EVER
> *Come up for air, then close your lips tightly and allow him to 'force' his way into your mouth.*

Sex immediately after a Hollywood wax has got to be my best ever. It hurt like hell having all my pubic hair removed, but it was worth it. You can feel everything. My husband was pretty impressed, too.
Rosa, 40

Defer his gratification. Lick his thighs and belly and give him a wicked look before opening your mouth... and moving onto his cock. Cover your teeth with your lips and gently begin to lick and suck. Some men like a lot of suction, others very little. Short, side-to-side licks will get him 110% hard.

Use your hands as well as your mouth. Make a ring around the base of his penis with your thumb and forefinger. This lengthens the tunnel of your mouth, and gives you control – think of it as a brake in case he gets carried away.

Some men love having their balls sucked. Others hate it. Gently lick and suck to see what flips his switch. If his moans are encouraging, take one of his balls in your mouth and gently hum for a real best-ever buzz.

You should be able to tell when he's about to come – he'll either slow down or speed up, and his moans will vary. But you might want to agree an advance warning like a tap on the head. Only swallow if you want to. It's a huge turn on to see you take it down, but he shouldn't pressure you to. If you don't want to, ask him to come over your breasts or stomach.

Deep throating – where the man inserts his penis deep into his partner's mouth – is another thing that's popular in porn films but is better to watch than to try. If you do want to experiment, here's how. She needs to be in a position where her head and her throat are in line, either with her head hanging off the bed or propped up on pillows. This makes a straight line of her throat, and prevents him feeling his penis has to bend around in her throat. He needs to progress slowly, allowing her to accommodate his dick little by little, and he needs to be sympathetic to the fact that she has to breathe through the gag reflex.

The best cunnilingus ever!

Cunnilingus is the clinical-sounding Latin name for oral sex performed on a woman. Going down on her, licking her out – call it what you want, done right it's the most sure-fire way to bring a woman to orgasm.

Build up to it – like normal sex, this needs foreplay. Most women find they can't take direct clitoral stimulation until they're warmed up.

The most common position for this is the woman lying back while the man kneels or lies between her legs. This offers the advantage of him being able to see exactly what he's doing, while she can just lie back and enjoy the delicious sensations. If you're into anal play, and she's confident about her ass and thighs, she can kneel on all fours while he lies on his back between her legs.

As ever, all women have different preferences. You should be able to gauge from the tone of her moans whether you're doing it for her. If she's too shy to tell you what she wants, get her to kiss your palm the way she wants to be kissed on her vagina.

Place your hand over her pubic bone and pull upwards slightly, so that her clit. is exposed. Start by kissing her labia the same way you'd kiss her lips. Start with your tongue soft on her clitoris. Whirl your tongue around the sensitive skin surrounding the bud rather than going straight for it. Don't use your tongue as a

BEST TIPS EVER

Apply the love-bite sucking sensation on the soft flesh of her pubic bone. This will stimulate the deeper layers of the clitoral tissue, which fan out for several centimetres around the bud itself.

mini-penis and thrust it in and out of her. Cunnilingus is a treat because it focuses on the clitoris, not the vagina.

The French have over 20 different words for kissing.

Make her think you've got all the time in the world – remember that while twenty minutes is the average time it takes for a woman to reach orgasm, some can take longer. If she thinks you're watching the clock, she'll feel under pressure and won't be able to enjoy herself.

Don't neglect the rest of her body. Her breasts, stomach, thighs and even hair are all crying out for your hands.

Maintain a slow, steady rhythm. Maintain a slow, steady rhythm. We've said it loud and we've said it twice because this is crucial to best-ever oral. It might be boring, but consistency is the key to making her come. Keep up that rhythm right to the end. Even when she's seconds away from climax, her orgasm could vanish if you suddenly change pace.

A lot of women are hung up about the way they smell down there. Truth is, the pheromones created in that part of the body are an aphrodisiac. Take a breather to reassure her that she smells, and tastes, delicious. The more relaxed and turned on she is, the more likely she is to come. If you're hung up, too, then a) why? and b) dribble a little runny honey on her clitoris to act as a natural lubricant and sweeten the experience for both of you.

Only 0.05% of men can give themselves fellatio. The rest would if they could.

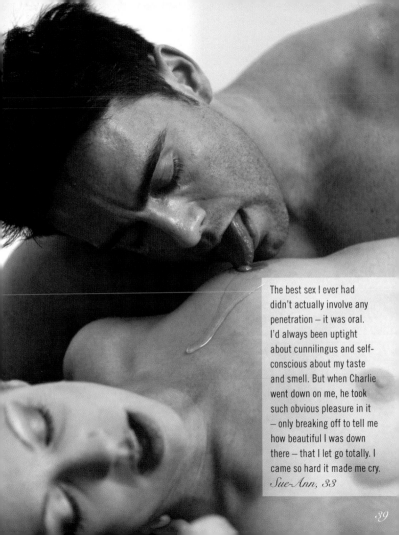

The best sex I ever had didn't actually involve any penetration — it was oral. I'd always been uptight about cunnilingus and self-conscious about my taste and smell. But when Charlie went down on me, he took such obvious pleasure in it — only breaking off to tell me how beautiful I was down there — that I let go totally. I came so hard it made me cry.

Sue-Ann, 33

39

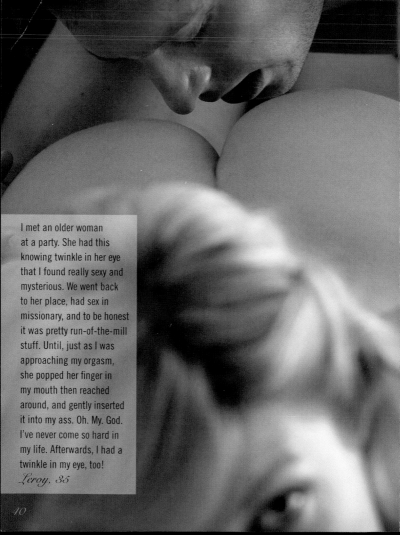

I met an older woman at a party. She had this knowing twinkle in her eye that I found really sexy and mysterious. We went back to her place, had sex in missionary, and to be honest it was pretty run-of-the-mill stuff. Until, just as I was approaching my orgasm, she popped her finger in my mouth then reached around, and gently inserted it into my ass. Oh. My. God. I've never come so hard in my life. Afterwards, I had a twinkle in my eye, too!

Leroy, 35

Best Ever...
Oral Tips for Him & Her

🐛 Make sure you're both shower-fresh before you start, but don't wash away any natural juices, ladies.

🐛 Vary the techniques you use – from lapping like at an ice cream to poking with a hard tongue to swirling and sucking, flicking and even humming.

🐛 Have a glass of water to hand to refresh your mouth if you get tired. Experiment with other drinks, too. Take a sip of champagne before giving your lover a special kiss and let the bubbles do the work. Vary the temperature of your mouth by swigging a cup of tea or an iced drink before going down on him.

🐛 Try rimming – the fine art of using the tongue to stimulate the anus. Begin with soft licks along the perineum (the skin between her vagina and anus, or between his balls and bum) and gauge your partner's reaction. If the moans are encouraging, stiffen your tongue and gently probe further.

🐛 Trim your pubic hair before oral sex – it's easier for your partner to pleasure you if they don't have to bite their way through layers of undergrowth. Guys, shave beforehand so you don't scratch her delicate skin. If you have a beard, soften it with hair conditioner first.

🐛 Enjoy yourself, whether you're giving or receiving. And afterwards, don't forget to tell your lover how good he/she tasted and smelled.

🐛 You are what you eat. Just as smoking, alcohol or spicy food can give you bad breath, they can also have a negative effect on the way you taste down below. Changing your diet to include lots of fresh fruit makes ladies sweet and juicy and semen taste fresh and appetising.

Best ever = *safest ever*

You can't relax and have red-hot sex if you're worried about catching a sexually transmitted disease. And you certainly can't perform in the bedroom if your genitals are in agony because of a bug you've picked up. So unless you're in a monogamous relationship and you've both been given a clean bill of health from the GUM clinic, condoms are essential. And make sure you always use one that's passed the safety test – the British Kitemark in the UK. The green bobbly one from the pub vending machine may be very amusing and give interesting sensations, but if it's not been tested to protect you from infection, what's the point? Okay, lecture over. Here's how to make it sexy.

🖤 *Don't* tear the condom out of its packet with your teeth. It looks very wild, but you might tear the rubber, too.

🖤 *Do* squeeze the air out of the teat at the top of the condom. This limits your chances of the rubber tearing, or the condom falling off.

🖤 *Don't* put it straight in; continue the massage while he's wearing the condom.

🖤 *Do* learn how to do it with your mouth. Make sure you're not wearing lipgloss or balm, as they can break down the latex. Give him oral sex to get him hard (*see page 32*). Cover your teeth with your lips – you don't want to nick the latex, or indeed his dick. Place the teat between your lips, holding it there with very light suction. Hold the shaft of his penis in one hand and place the condom over it. Use your tongue and lips to roll it all the way down. It's a technique that takes a while to master, but once mastered, is never forgotten – by the giver or the recipient!

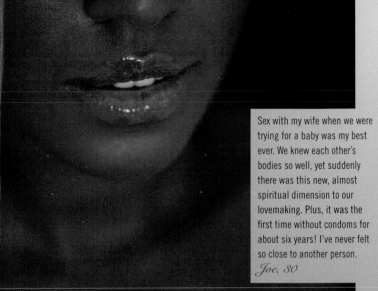

Sex with my wife when we were trying for a baby was my best ever. We knew each other's bodies so well, yet suddenly there was this new, almost spiritual dimension to our lovemaking. Plus, it was the first time without condoms for about six years! I've never felt so close to another person.

Joe, 30

BEST TIPS EVER

Even your usual position suddenly becomes spicier when you vary the location. Play a little game where you list your favourite positions and some fantasy locations, then put all the names in a hat. One of you pulls out the position, the other the place...the creativity and challenge involved will get that all-important blood pumping around your bodies.

Best...
Positions
...Ever

There are 62 sex positions listed in the world's oldest and most famous sex manual, the Kama Sutra. They're challenging, demanding and while it can be fun to try them out – like a giant game of sex twister – they don't all necessarily lead to good sex.

For best-ever sex, you only need a handful of tried-and-tested positions. There's a reason the following positions are the most popular ones in the world. They are, quite simply, the ones that research and experience proves get the orgasmic results you're after. If you want to take your lovemaking to the next level, then these are the only positions you'll ever need.

We tend to start with one position and stay with it all the way through any one session. Why limit yourself? You can make different shapes depending on what your bodies crave at any stage of lovemaking. Feel free to have a five-minute break for more foreplay or even a cup of tea halfway through before switching to another position for your finale.

The biggest-ever filmed orgy, comprising 500 couples, took place in Japan in October 2006.

1. The She-Ra
Best female orgasm ever!

Why it's the best-ever: Penetrative sex is delicious, but the fact remains that it's clitoral stimulation, not vaginal penetration, that delivers the most female orgasms. This position offers the visual treat and the deep penetration he loves and leaves the clitoris accessible for stimulation with his or her fingers, or a sex toy. The woman-on-top position also means that she retains the power and control throughout – which can be a huge aphrodisiac in itself.

BEST TIPS EVER

Sex during pregnancy can be awkward and uncomfortable as old favourites like the missionary are impossible. The She-Ra is comfortable for her and lets him adore her lush body.

How to do it: He lies on his back – he may find it more comfortable with his head propped on pillows or resting in his cradled hands. She straddles him and gently slides herself down onto his erection and uses her thighs to move up and down. Both partners have access to her breasts and clitoris and he can use his hands to guide her hips into the rhythm he likes. This is a physically undemanding position for him – he doesn't have to support his or her weight, so he can concentrate on the steady clitoral stimulation she needs to reach orgasm. And because he can't control the thrusting, he'll last a little longer than man-on-top or rear-entry positions. The only drawback? Unless she has strong thighs, this can get a little tiring for her.

2. The Cat
Best simultaneous orgasm ever!

Why it's the best ever: This incredible position has nothing to do with feline slinkiness but is short for the Coital Alignment Technique. It's a new approach to intercourse based on pressure and rocking motions rather than the in-out thrusting that most of us are used to. Women are three times – that's *three times* – more likely to orgasm with this revolutionary position than any other. It works by delaying his orgasm, because he's not thrusting but rocking, and giving her the slow, slow, steady, steady clit stimulation she needs to come. Although you need to concentrate, it's actually very physically undemanding. No position gets better orgasms with less work!

★ BEST TIPS EVER
Make a mix of your favourite long, slow, sexy tunes and see how long you can last. Rocking in time to sexy music can help you concentrate, and take the pressure off to perfect this unusual technique.

How to do it: He gets on top of her, as in the missionary, and lines his pelvis up over hers. His penis is inside, but he's riding high so the base of his penis is just outside her vagina, and his pubic bone is pressing down on her pubic hair. She wraps her legs around his thighs and rests her ankles on his calves. They then move just their pelvises, not their arms or legs, pushing up and down against other. Rather than thrusting they move in small circular massaging motions.

3. One-Minute Wonder
Best quickie ever!

Why it's the best ever: Quickie sex is special – it lends itself to those times when you've been sharing fantasies, flirting all day or just for horny mornings when you have to be out the door in five minutes but you have to have each other right now. You need a position that's as intense and energetic as the waves of lust you're both feeling, one that's dramatic and demanding (it's worth having a bit of lube to hand just in case her body's juices can't keep up with the frantic pace).

How to do it: She sits on a surface about the same height as his pelvis – so kitchen worktops, bedroom furniture, sinks or even office cabinets are ideal. She wraps her legs around his back, while he penetrates her. If she crosses her legs behind his back, she can dig her heels into his buttocks, pushing him deeper and deeper into her. Her weight is supported, allowing her to relax in his arms and surrender to the deep penetration and if he grinds the base of his dick into her clitoris, she'll find that her sexual response speeds up. If she wants to express her orgasm even more, she can hold a mini vibrator against her clit. This position lends itself to sex fully clothed: all it takes is for her to pull her panties to one side and for him to unbuckle his belt and the hot, urgent lovemaking can begin.

⭐ BEST TIPS EVER

You can try it up against the wall if you want a workout for his back and her legs, but this can draw the body's energy away from the pelvis and diminish the sensations there, so this advanced version is for those times when you're both seconds away from your climax.

The best sex for me is the lazy, sunny sex you have in the middle of the daytime. Weekdays are best, because everyone else is at work. Sex in the evening is fine, but making the world stand still in the middle of the day is really special. Foreplay can last for hours, which means the resulting orgasms are *amazing*.
Lisa, 21

To me, the best-ever
sex always comes
about six months
into a relationship.
If you've made it that
far, then the feelings
are pretty intense,
and you know each
other's bodies well
enough to please
each other without
being asked.
Benjamin, 29

4. Yab Yum
Best spiritual connection ever!

Why it's the best ever: Sometimes it's nice to connect with your lover on a level that's deeper than the purely physical. This position is step one on the road to tantric sex, which is as much about making a spiritual connection with your lover as anything else. It's about her orgasm, more than his. The focus is on togetherness and prolonging the pleasure rather than rushing towards orgasm. During it, synchronise your breathing – in ancient Indian lore, you are literally breathing in each other's very being and you will feel closer with every breath.

How to do it: He kneels or sits with his legs crossed while she wraps her arms around his neck and her legs around his waist, and gently takes his erection inside her. Keep eye contact and breathing in time. For as long as possible, the woman keeps up just enough pelvic movement for him to stay hard inside her. She can squeeze her PC muscles (*see page 94*). The emphasis here is on delaying his orgasm – if he looks like he's coming, she can raise her legs over his shoulders. This offers her deeper penetration, but the angle of her vagina means that the tip of his penis – the bit that's likely to make him come when stimulated – is not getting too much attention. After you've both climaxed, remain in the position, continuing to breathe in harmony, until he is totally limp.

BEST TIPS EVER
Make this a shared experience in more ways than one. Share food and wine before you make love, and don't be afraid to break off to re-fuel midway through. The longer you make the experience last, the deeper your connection.

5. Missionary
Best intimacy ever!

Why it's the best ever: This is the most popular sex position in the world for a reason. It isn't new, it isn't ground-breaking, and it isn't fashionable – in fact, many people regard man-on-top sex as boring and unadventurous. But there will always be something deeply romantic, comforting and intimate about this position. It's powerfully erotic, with the woman vulnerable and the man able to exercise his full sexual power. As the woman doesn't need to exert herself, it can be a great position to switch to after woman-on-top sex.

How to do it: She lies on her back with her legs parted. He lies over her, supporting his weight on his elbows, enters her, and thrusts. He controls the depth and speed of the penetration. Kissing and talking is possible throughout, and the all-over full-frontal body contact is an extension of foreplay. Clitoral stimulation is possible in this position, although you do have to work at it. She can wriggle around and buck her hips until she finds an angle that allows the base of his penis to caress and grind against her clitoris. If she puts a pillow under her hips, you're more likely to make this connection. It alters the whole tilt of her pelvis, exposing her clitoris to much more friction.

⭐ BEST TIPS EVER

If he slips on a vibrating cock ring (see page 90), he literally becomes a sex toy: the tiny buzz attached to his cock will tease her clitoris, and the cock ring will harden his erection.

BEST TIPS EVER

Juxtapose the driving intensity of the penetration with some gentle stimulation elsewhere on your bodies. Tickle each other's nipples, arms and lips with a long-stemmed peacock feather as you make love.

6. The Flower Press
Best deep penetration ever!

Why it's the best-ever: This man-on-top position maximises the size of his penis so it's great if his penis is much smaller than her vagina. It's the best way to get the intense, deep penetration many couples crave without using a rear-entry position which many women feel is impersonal. It's visually stimulating for both partners: she can watch him in a position of power and domination above her, while he gets the highly charged erotic thrill of seeing her spread open beneath him, while he slides in and out of her wetness.

How to do it: He kneels on the bed and she lies back and brings her knees right up to her chin, so that when he enters her, her feet are at either side of his head or resting on his chest. He holds onto her thighs or shins, and she grabs onto his hips. Her pelvis really tilts up, allowing for the deepest penetration in a man-on-top position. The closer she draws her knees to her chest, the deeper he'll go, and the bigger he'll feel inside her. The intensity of this position carries the risk of premature ejaculation. If it looks like he's going to climax too soon, she can slide her hands in between his legs and gently tug on his balls, which will delay his orgasm. Or, if she wants to encourage his climax, she can press gently on his perineum – the patch of skin between his balls and bum – which will stimulate his prostate gland and trip him over the edge into orgasm.

Your average man has seven erections a day. You can put at least one to good use, surely?

7. Doggy Style
Best G-spot stimulation ever!

Why it's the best ever: For women who know that the G-spot exists because they have the orgasms to prove it, this simple, primal position is the best way for his dick to stroke that front wall of her vagina where it's located. For women who aren't sure, this is perhaps the most enjoyable way to find out. It offers snug penetration for him and overwhelming fullness for her. Aside from these benefits, it's also really easy for her to stimulate her clit with her hands, or a toy, without having to disturb the rhythm of his thrusts.

How to do it: She kneels on all fours, her legs slightly parted. He kneels behind her, his hands on her hips, and penetrates her and thrusts hard. It can be so overwhelming that he might want to start with one or two gentle thrusts before building up to the pounding that most people love this position for. That goes double if he's really big.

My best-ever sex position is doggy style. I love to talk dirty, but I'm too self-conscious to do it when we're face to face. But when he's fucking me from behind, I can let rip with whatever fantasies come into my head. There's something so raw and animalistic about it.
Roxanne, 25

This is the most common rear-entry position for lots of good reasons. Although he controls penetration, she can move in time with him, pushing down and backwards to lengthen the walls of her vagina, or tilting her hips forward to tighten it and make penetration feel snugger for both of them. He can see himself entering her, a huge visual treat. The downsides? Not all women are able to locate their G-spots, and can become disheartened. If this is the case, take the pressure off yourself and simply enjoy the position for its depth and urgency.

★ BEST TIPS EVER

If you've always wanted to indulge in dirty talk, but feel too shy, doggy-style sex is the ideal position to let rip. The animalistic nature of the position encourages you to howl whatever comes into your mind — and because you don't have eye contact with each other, you can say explicit, arousing things you wouldn't dare to face-to-face.

BEST TIPS EVER

This position is heavily weighted in favour of the woman's pleasure. Nothing wrong with that, but if she squeezes her PC muscles in a rapid fluttering motion around his dick, she can massage him to an intense orgasm that will stop him feeling neglected!

8. Come again
Best multiple orgasms ever!

Why it's the best ever: So what is a multiple orgasm? Essentially, it's when a woman reaches climax, but afterwards instead of going into recovery mode, she hovers around the plateau stage, ready to receive even more pleasure. It won't happen for everyone, but this position combines the three factors most likely to make it happen – clitoral stimulation, full-body contact and varying degrees of penetration.

How to do it: He lies back while she lowers herself onto him. Then she draws her legs up so her knees are parallel with her chest. She controls the position of her pelvis, so she can make sure her clit is in line with his pubic bone, and because he can't thrust, she can manipulate the movements to suit her needs. (His inability to thrust also means that he will come slower, so it's great if he suffers from premature ejaculation.) By drawing her legs up towards her chest, she can alter the angle and depth of her vagina, making it much more likely that his penis will stimulate her G-spot. Orgasm is reached by gently rocking over him. He should hold off orgasm until hers has been achieved. Then, if she's able to climax again, penetration can continue. The trick with multiple orgasms is to keep stimulation varied and not to over-arouse any one area. The minute she's climaxed from clitoral stimulation, he removes his attention from her genitals and immediately begins to stimulate her breast, neck, lips, or anywhere else she likes to be touched.

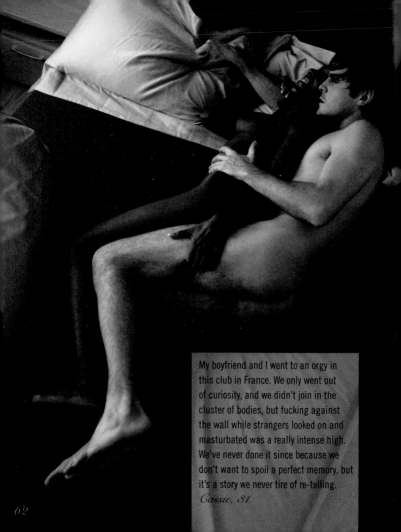

My boyfriend and I went to an orgy in this club in France. We only went out of curiosity, and we didn't join in the cluster of bodies, but fucking against the wall while strangers looked on and masturbated was a really intense high. We've never done it since because we don't want to spoil a perfect memory, but it's a story we never tire of re-telling.

Cassie, 31

9. Spoons
Best sleepy sex ever!

Why it's the best-ever: The opposite of the energetic quickie is lazy, snuggly sex at the end of the day. Whether you're watching an erotic film together on the sofa or drifting off to sleep in each other's arms, the spoons position gets maximum results with minimum exertion from either partner. It's the best cure for insomnia we know. You don't even have to change positions to fall asleep in each others' arms.

How to do it: She lies on her side while he snuggles up behind her. She then draws up her knees a little and opens her thighs while he tucks his knees behind her, entering her from the rear. With his arms wrapped around her he can pleasure her whole body. He's effectively continuing foreplay even when he's inside her, indulging the super-sensitive erogenous zones around the neck, ears and shoulders, whether that's with a massage or nuzzling and kissing. No position better lends itself to him whispering sweet nothings in her ear. The only downside is that if his penis is much smaller than her vagina, or you both like deep penetration, this position can feel a little shallow.

BEST TIPS EVER

To make access to her clitoris easier, she can wrap her uppermost leg back over her partner's, and pleasure herself manually or with a vibrator. She can then return his favours by reaching through his legs and tugging or stroking his balls.

10. The Rosebud
Best full-body orgasms ever!

Why it's the best ever: 10% of women can orgasm just through having their breasts caressed, and stimulating all the erogenous zones (rather than just the ones located at the hip) can make the difference between a straightforward clitoral/penile orgasm and a tingly, long-lasting, all-over body orgasm that perfectly illustrates the difference between good and great sex. In this position, almost no inch of skin is left unstimulated. Faces are close, arms, legs are entangled, bodies are pressed together and backs are receptive to caresses.

How to do it: Sit facing each other, with your legs crossed or wrapped around each other's backs. Then inch together until he's penetrating her and slowly rock your way to orgasm, stroking each other's backs or letting your nipples brush against each other. She's bearing down on his penis with all her weight, making for deep and massaging penetration. Being on top, she calls the shots on the pace and depth – he doesn't have to do very much. Because her legs are spread, the skin around her clitoris is exposed, stretched and even more sensitive to his touch. It's good for kissing. It can be hard to balance, but that's only an excuse to hold on to each other super tight. The man may feel frustrated that he can't thrust though the visual show at eye level should make up for this.

⭐ BEST TIPS EVER

If you're curious about bondage, this position is an intimate and unthreatening way to experiment with levels of restraint. Fasten one partner's hands together with a stocking and slip them over the other's head. You will literally be bound together in this position.

The first time I had sex was the best time. I've had more skilled sex since, and stronger orgasms, but you can't beat the thrill of entering this whole new dimension. Finding out what it felt like to put my dick in a woman was as exhilarating as suddenly finding out that I could fly!

Christopher, 27

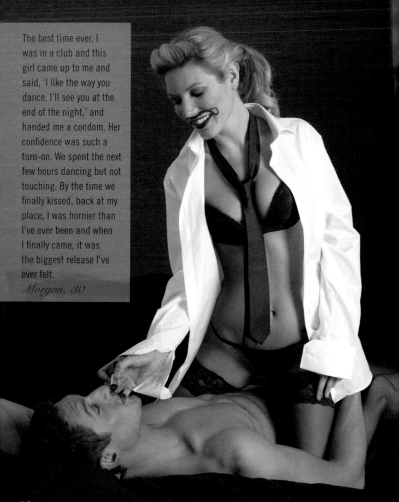

The best time ever, I was in a club and this girl came up to me and said, 'I like the way you dance. I'll see you at the end of the night,' and handed me a condom. Her confidence was such a turn-on. We spent the next few hours dancing but not touching. By the time we finally kissed, back at my place, I was hornier than I've ever been and when I finally came, it was the biggest release I've ever felt.
Morgan, 30

Best...
Fantasies
...Ever

Sexual fantasies are the thoughts you have while you're masturbating, erotic dreams, even things you think to get yourself in the mood while you're with your partner. They can be as simple as a single image or long, involved scenarios with a cast of characters and a detailed (and dirty) plot.

It's possible to arouse yourself using only your mind – men can have erections, women get wet, and a lucky few people can actually bring themselves to orgasm through the power of their own imaginations alone.

Many people are ashamed of their sex fantasies because they involve someone other than their partner, or they involve social taboos they wouldn't really want in real life – for example, group sex or gay sex. But the whole point is that they're only fantasies, and a place to let your sexual imagination run wild. A lot of people – women and men – have fantasies about being overpowered during sex. This does not mean they want to be attacked by a thug in an alleyway – it's about abandoning responsibility, letting go of guilt and surrendering to your wildest sexual urges.

A word of warning: if something's really troubling you – it's affecting your relationship, you can't get aroused without thinking about it, or you're worried it might be crossing into dangerous or even illegal areas – then get professional help. Contact the British Association for Counselling and Psychotherapy for a registered therapist who can help with your problems.

His top ten

1. Sex with an anonymous woman
2. Sex with two women at once (one of whom is his partner)
3. Watching other people have sex
4. Other people watching him have sex
5. Sex with a prostitute
6. Sex with another man
7. Being dominated
8. Group sex
9. Watching another man have sex with his partner
10. Being tied up during sex

Her top ten

1. Sex with her partner
2. Sex with another woman
3. Sex with a stranger
4. Sex with a celebrity, friend, acquaintance or colleague
5. Sex before an audience
6. Watching another couple make love
7. Being tied up or restrained during sex
8. Sex as a 'punishment'
9. Sex with a faceless, anonymous man
10. Group sex

The best sex I ever had was with another woman. We both knew exactly how to make each other come, and it went on for hours – unlike hetero sex, lesbian sex isn't over when the man orgasms. Plus, the softness of her skin, her lips and breasts, were a revelation. It made me realise how fluid our sexuality is.
Michele, 33

Role with it

Some fantasies work best when kept as a delicious, private secret, but sharing your favourite fantasy with your partner can super-size your sex life. Role play means that you both acknowledge it's just a game but you can still lose yourselves in it. You'll be united in the psychological bond as well as the physical act – a sizzling short cut to your best sex ever.

Raise the subject with sensitivity. Remember, the essence of role play is that you're pretending to be someone you're not – but taking this too literally will mean you and your partner become detached or feel excluded. For example, your lover won't like it if you say you want to sleep with your boss. But if you tell him you're turned on by authority and power (which is what the boss fantasy is ultimately all about) and suggest he spanks you over a desk, while he wears a suit and you wear nothing, then you're involving him in a non-threatening role-play scenario that he's much more likely to go for.

Role play – The Rules

Change the way you look. It lets you slip into character and gives your partner a visual jolt, as though they're meeting you for the first time. Wigs are great for this.

94% of women would dress up to spice up their sex lives.

Use props. For example, get a cane from a toyshop if you're acting out a teacher /pupil fantasy. Props, like costumes, remind you that this isn't normal lovemaking, they encourage you to get creative, and they also give you something to hide behind if you feel self-conscious at first.

I love sex by candlelight. There's something historical and romantic about flickering church candles – plus, it's really flattering. We can both see just enough to get turned on, but not so much that we're self-conscious. Perfect!

Deanna, 40

Change your environment. The more familiar you are with your same old bed, the harder it'll be to lose yourself in a fantasy. If you're in your bedroom, dress it up. You don't have to spend a fortune. Dark sheets at the window with candles on the floor can create a sexy dungeon. Sprinkling the bed with rose petals can really enhance a romantic fantasy. Better still, take your role-play on location. Book a hotel room or drive your car to a remote spot and get busy there.

Get into character. If you always drink white wine and listen to rock, knock back a courvoisier on ice with sexy R'n'B blaring. If your role-play is historical, listen to music from that period. Watch a movie or read a book that sums up the atmosphere you want to create. It doesn't *have* to be an erotic one...

Try something new – a position or technique from this book. Make sure it's something outside your usual repertoire. It's exciting to know that your 'character' has some moves that you don't.

When the role play is over, agree on a code word or phrase that means you can tap into your experience again whenever you want. For example, if you've experimented with games of control and restraint, the word 'ribbons' whispered innocently across the table at a dinner party will transport you and your partner back to the private game you shared... and get you both hot for a repeat performance.

⭐ BEST TIPS EVER

Have a plan. Think about the kind of language your character would use, have a few sexy lines up your sleeve. You should find that the moment carries you along, but if one of you gets an attack of the nerves, then having a 'script' can ease you back into the fantasy.

1. Sex worker

Like most role-play games, this is about power and submission. The partner paying for sex is 'buying' control, obedience and power. The partner playing the part of the sex worker is letting go of socially acceptable ideas and allowing themselves to become a sex object for one night only. Everything about this scenario is forbidden – that's why it's so powerful.

Play it safe. Book a cheap room in a seedy hotel in a seaside town. Bring a wad of Monopoly money with you. The sex worker 'refuses' to comply with any sexual requests until she or he is paid – that could be £100 for oral sex, £100 for masturbation, and £200 for full sex. Work your way through as many favours as possible before making love on a bed strewn with 'cash'.

A walk on the wild side. The partner playing the sex worker dresses the part – she can wear a fur coat and no knickers, he can wear the sharp suit of the American gigolo – and waits on the street. The 'client' drives by, winds down the window and opens the car door. Fast, anonymous sex on the back seat follows (if the woman is playing the sex worker in this scenario, the man should never let her out of his sight).

2. Swapping roles

This is about exploring the other side of your sexuality. Society often dictates that men should be sex machines, always horny and able to perform, while women ought to be softer, more submissive and should react to their partner's desires rather than being guided by their own passions. The truth is, we all have elements of so-called masculine and feminine within us. Gender-swap fantasies are a great way to explore the complex levels of our sexualities.

Play it safe. In the privacy of your own bedroom, dress each other for your new roles. He can 'shave' her with an empty razor, while she can put make-up on his face. She can slouch around in his boxers and suit jacket while he wears her lingerie and stockings. Once the transformation is complete, the clothes can come off again as you make love. Are you drawn to different positions in your new roles? Do you want to be more vocal, or softer, than usual? Let your new personality rule.

A walk on the wild side. Dress in your transgender clothes and go public: either to a sex club or even just out to dinner. Enjoy the curious stares of members of the public. Back home, experiment with different styles of intercourse. She can wear a strap-on dildo and penetrate him anally – she gets to experience the power of penetration, while he allows his body to be passive and receive her 'penis'.

3. Film stars

Whether you get off on watching people, or you want to be watched, filming yourselves making love is an increasingly popular fantasy – and one that's never been easier to act out. Wouldn't it be great to watch an erotic movie when, just for once, you can be 100% sure that the 'actors' weren't faking their orgasms?

Play it safe. If you're not sure about performing on camera, start with a series of still

My confidence was really low after my divorce. Then I met a guy online, and after a few dates we made love. I was so nervous, but he was so hot for my body that he boosted my self-esteem and unleashed this tigress in me. At the age of 41, I realised what all the fuss was about. Sex has got better ever since — but that first time was the turning point.
Lindsey, 44

photographs – do a striptease for your lover, allowing them to take one photograph each time you remove an item of clothing. Or simply pose naked, and get used to the feeling of being vulnerable before the camera. Who knows, you might uncover an exhibitionist side you never suspected lurked within you.

A walk on the wild side. Take your movie on location. Give it a title, a plot, script it, get some props and costumes in. Do it in character – method act, behaving like the slutty housewife or strict master for a few days in the run-up to your filming session. Nervous about your screen debut? Lick champagne off each other's skin to take the edge off your stage fright. Pamper each other beforehand – massage rich body lotion into each other so you know your bodies look their best. Discuss the positions you plan to use, and the order you'll do them in. But don't be afraid to vary it and ad lib if the mood takes over...

4. Group sex

Group sex fantasies – whether that's a threesome or a full-on orgy with dozens of bodies writhing in a room – are perennially popular. They offer something for the voyeur as well as the exhibitionist, and are potentially the ultimate in taboo-busting abandonment. However, the realities of human emotions – not to mention the health risks – mean that this is one scenario many people prefer to leave to pornography or fantasy rather than carry over into reality.

Play it safe. You can recreate the thrill of watching others have sex while performing yourself by making love in front of a group sex DVD. This offers all the thrills with none of the risks. To spice it up even more, surround yourselves and your TV set with opposing mirrors, so your images are reflecting back at you dozens of times – you can see yourselves making love, and you become both performer and audience.

A walk on the wild side. Sure you can both handle the potential jealousies of group sex? Then lay down rules. Choose your partners carefully – a reputable sex club rather than random pervs from the internet – and make sure you all know how far you're prepared to go. Do you just want to watch and kiss, or are you prepared to have intercourse with other people in front of each other? Sexual health is more important here than ever. Caress who you like, but don't swap bodily fluids with anyone – that means condoms for full sex, dental dams for oral, and common sense at all times. And the usual rule about never doing anything you don't want to goes double here.

62% of women have watched pornography with their man.

The best sex I ever had was in the bathroom. My girlfriend did that thing where you angle two mirrors so that the reflection goes on forever, and we had sex standing up in between them. Every angle was covered, and seeing myself penetrate her dozens of times was something I'll never forget.

Jake, 31

The best sex I ever had took place the summer I lived in New York. My apartment was on the fifth floor and one time when the elevator broke, my date and I had to walk up 90 stairs. By the time we got to the top we were hot, really sweaty and out of breath. There was something so primal and sultry about it, we barely made it through the front door.

Janis, 29

Power trip – best-ever bondage

Both men and women fantasise about being restrained, or tying up their partner, during sex. This is called B.D.S.M. – which stands for Bondage, Domination, Sadism and Masochism – in sex clubs. The appeal is about the illusion of helplessness, and the surrender that it involves. If you've got issues about guilt, it can be wonderfully liberating to surrender your body to your lover's control. Some people love to dominate their partner and get off on making them come – others want to submit to their partner's every whim. It can be an outlet for the feelings of sexual power, rivalry and frustration that we all experience.

Role-play games involving power deserve their own special little section, because they require an extra element of trust. You are, literally, putting your body in your partner's hands. For this reason it's a bad idea to go back and play B.D.S.M. games with a total stranger you met in a club, no matter how cute he or she is.

The first question to ask yourself is whether you're in charge (the master, mistress, dominatrix, top, or dom) or you want to surrender (the slave, servant, sub, or bottom). Most of us naturally lean towards one or the other, but if you're not sure, picture yourself in two scenarios: in one, you're standing over your partner's prone body while they quiver with desire and call you master or mistress (dom). In the other, you're the one lying tied up and at their mercy (sub). One of them should get your heart beating a little faster than the other.

BEST TIPS EVER

Do agree what you will and won't do before you start, especially if you're new to this. Agree where the limits are, and don't push them this time. You can always go further later.

People think it's about pain. Light slaps and lashes with a whip can be part of it, but B.D.S.M. really boils down to control and surrender. Begin with mental bondage. The sub lies on the bed with no physical restraints but under the dom's command. The sub may not move a muscle of his or her body without express permission from the dom, and must do whatever the dom instructs – whether that's to spread your legs, raise your ass in the air, perform oral sex, masturbate or simply to close your eyes. This is a great way to explore your new personas without the expense or commitment of investing in physical props.

The next step is to tie the sub to the bedposts. If you're already in love with the idea of B.D.S.M., then invest in a pair of handcuffs or leg restraints from a specialist sex shop. Or, if you're still taking things slowly, try using a pair of tights or stockings as restraints. They're softer and less threatening. When the sub is tied up tight, the dom can leave the room for ten minutes, leaving the slave to experience a delicious build-up of sexual tension.

Bondage tape, available from sex shops, is a safe and versatile toy. It sticks to itself, but not to your skin, and can be used to bind arms and legs or round and round the body to gift-wrap it, leaving peep-holes for nipples, penises or clitorises.

Do try a little light pain. Try tickling before moving onto spanking. It's a fun, safe way to experiment with feelings of helplessness. When you're spanking, stick to the ass and thighs, *never* the back or abdomen as this is where your vital organs are.

Don't play BDSM games when you're drunk or on drugs. Your judgement's impaired and you could end up hurting yourself or your partner, going further than you would sober, or even choking to death.

Do have a safe word that means stop. B.D.S.M. games often involve people pretending to be tortured, so the 'slave' might be crying, 'No, master, make it stop' while really she's thinking, 'Hmm, I might come in a minute'. Choose neutral words that have no sexual connotations like 'traffic light', 'blue', or 'rose'. Don't be afraid to say if you're freaking out. We all have our limits – part of the fun of BDSM is finding out where yours is. And part of the responsibility and trust implicit in playing the game is stopping when your partner says so.

I was nervous about letting my boyfriend blindfold me during sex. Now I wonder why I waited so long. It's astonishing how much more alive your body becomes when your primary sense is limited. I came in the missionary position with almost no clit stimulation – that's how turned on I was.
Claire, 28

Best...
Toys
...Ever

The best sex I ever have is solo; I love having the house to myself, having a glass of wine and then settling down on the sofa with a really dirty fetish story in one hand and my Rampant Rabbit in the other.

Emmy, 29

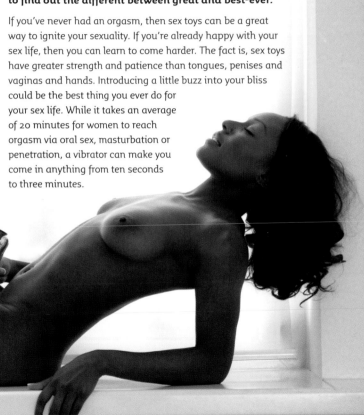

Think you're having great sex? If you've never introduced toys into your lovemaking, you're about to find out the different between great and best-ever.

If you've never had an orgasm, then sex toys can be a great way to ignite your sexuality. If you're already happy with your sex life, then you can learn to come harder. The fact is, sex toys have greater strength and patience than tongues, penises and vaginas and hands. Introducing a little buzz into your bliss could be the best thing you ever do for your sex life. While it takes an average of 20 minutes for women to reach orgasm via oral sex, masturbation or penetration, a vibrator can make you come in anything from ten seconds to three minutes.

The hottest sex I ever had was with a girlfriend who produced a vibrator from nowhere and wedged it between us. The buzzing sensation travelled through my dick and along my balls and it must have been directly on her clit, too, because she came about ten seconds later. The intensity of her orgasm squeezed my dick dry.
Dan, 22

Men can be a little bit jealous and suspicious of sex toys. Make sure you incorporate it into mutual stimulation and pleasure. It's important he realises this is an addition to the pleasure he already gives you, not a replacement for it.

So read on for the best-ever guide to the best-ever toys on the market.

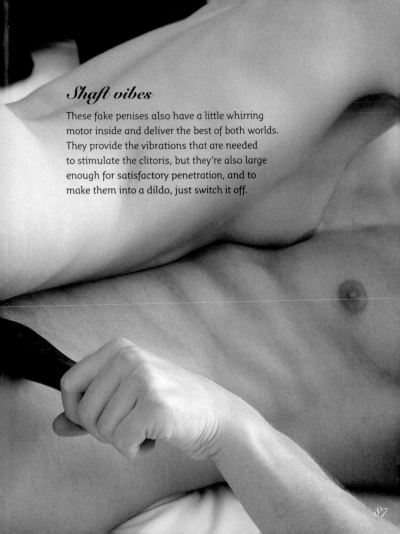

Shaft vibes

These fake penises also have a little whirring
motor inside and deliver the best of both worlds.
They provide the vibrations that are needed
to stimulate the clitoris, but they're also large
enough for satisfactory penetration, and to
make them into a dildo, just switch it off.

Clit stims

More women orgasm from clitoral stimulation than anything else (80% as opposed to 20% from penetration). Either clamp clit stims between your bits during sex in missionary, or use them during foreplay. Most clit stim vibes are small and can fit in your handbag. Hands-free vibes range from strap-on clit stims to mini bullet vibes encased in a pair of knickers that operate by remote control. This type can also be strapped onto a man just under his balls to make intercourse, masturbation or oral sex go with an extra buzz, stimulating his prostate gland through the outside of his body via the perineum.

The Rabbit

The shaft of the vibrator is filled with tiny internal balls that rotate at the flick of a switch to stimulate the inside of the vaginal wall and the G-spot. In addition, there are two little vibrating 'ears' (hence The Rabbit tag), which stimulate the clitoris. The highly efficient clit stim means The Rabbit is ideal for a warm-up before quickie sex – placing the ears against your clitoris for a few seconds will jump-start your body's arousal cycle and you'll start to lubricate, ready for a penis.

Dildos

These, the simplest (and oldest) sex toys are penis-shaped toys that don't vibrate, and are designed for penetrating the vagina and/or anus. They come in all shapes and sizes, from huge realistic flesh-coloured dicks complete with veins to glittery, bendy, brightly coloured ones.

Love eggs

Also known as Ben Wa Balls, these shiny round baubles are placed inside the vagina, where the vaginal walls automatically grip them. This trains your internal muscles to grip hard, meaning your orgasms will become stronger and your partner's penis will feel snugger inside you during vaginal intercourse. The more you move about, the more stimulated you'll be. Also good for G-spot location and stimulation.

Cock rings

Cock rings are designed to fit around the base of the penis and the scrotum, restricting blood flow. This stops your balls rising up into your body, which happens at the point of orgasm – so stops the orgasm until you remove the ring. They make erections harder and longer-lasting, and orgasm more intense.

Warning! Because you're talking about stopping blood flow, there are some ground rules. Never wear it for longer than 20 minutes, and take it off right away if it starts to hurt. Anyone with a history of circulatory problems, diabetes, nerve disorders, blood clots or anyone who's on blood-thinning medication should not use a cock ring.

Best couples toy ever!
Vibrating cock rings

These are usually made of soft silicone, either smooth or ridged, with a little vibrator attached that will run up against the woman's clitoris during intercourse while also vibrating his penis. It can make all the difference for the 50% of women who find it hard to reach orgasm through vaginal penetration alone. It effectively turns his penis into a vibrator that's inside her. It makes simultaneous orgasms more likely as well: speeding up her climax and slowing his down.

Sex toys – The Rules

The better you care for your toy, the longer it will last. Jelly and latex toys are cheap and come in bright, funky colours. Plastic and acrylic are smooth and hard to the touch. They're easy to clean but also cold and inflexible, which isn't always comfortable for penetration. Silicone are in the mid-price range, and are flexible enough to bend to your body's curves and warm up quickly. Cyberskin is a new material used in lifelike replicas of genitalia and as close to the real thing as you can get. However, these hi-tech toys can be a pain to keep clean.

Warning! Different materials are compatible with different lubes – check on the label, or ask your sex toy retailer if you're unsure. If you plan on using it in the shower (and if you don't, why not?) make sure it's a waterproof model.

Anal toys

Toys designed for backdoor lovin' have their own set of rules. The sex is dirty, but the toys stay clean. Bacteria live in the anus so follow the cleaning instructions properly and do use a condom. Never transfer a vibe from the anus to the vagina, clitoris, penis or mouth without washing it first, or putting a new condom on it. Always use lube. Unlike the vagina, the anus doesn't produce its own, natural lubrication (no matter how horny you get!). *Never* put anything up your ass that doesn't have a flared base – sex toys for the anus are shaped this way for a reason, to stop them disappearing altogether: easier than you'd think when you're excited and lubed up.

Love beads

These are a series of marble-sized plastic beads that are strung on a cord which is inserted into the anus. Before you use them, run your fingers up and down to check there are no sharp and potentially dangerous snags on the plastic moulding. Slowly insert them, one at a time and remove them as you approach your climax.

Once the beads are inside you, get your partner to rotate them very gently and very slowly, so that every inch of your rectum is stimulated. Experiment with fast and slow insertion and removal – try easing them out, or whipping them away at the moment of orgasm. See which one makes you come hardest.

Butt plugs

A butt plug is designed so that the prostate gland will be stimulated, but still allow you a degree of flexibility. Men can find that wearing a butt plug during penetrative sex can trigger the most intense orgasms ever as the prostrate gland is stimulated from within as well as externally. For orgasm overload, assume a kneeling position and masturbate while using your free hand to gently, slowly rotate the butt plug in your ass.

Although women don't have a prostate gland, many enjoy using butt plugs, especially those like the 'ponygirl', a plug with a miniature horsehair tail that's great for kitsch bedroom play.

Anal vibes

These super-slim vibrators are designed especially for the back passage. They will loosen up the sphincter (the muscle that surrounds the anus), making penetration with a penis, hand or larger sex toy much easier. Slipping a vibe in his anus during oral sex will tip him over the edge (and halve the time you have to spend doing the blow-job!).

And Finally...

The Best Best-Ever Sex Tip!

All of the advice I've given you should make your sex life better.
But for stronger orgasms, longer-lasting lust, increased desire
and greater confidence, you need to work out your genital
muscles – the ones that expand and contract so deliciously
when you climax. Men and women who regularly exercise
these muscles – known as the PC muscle – consistently report
stronger, longer orgasms. And the beauty of it is, you can do
this intimate workout as often as you like, every day, without
breaking a sweat.

The world's best-selling sex toy is the Rampant Rabbit, with well over two million sold.

For her

To locate your PC muscle, stop and start
the flow when you're peeing. The muscular
sensation you feel is your PC muscle working.
Put a finger in your vagina and squeeze and
you'll feel it working. Gradually build up to 20
contractions a day.

Supersize your sexercise. Put a slim
vibrator or dildo inside your vagina and see if
you can move it in and out just using your PC

muscle. Clenching your PC muscle should make you feel as though you're trying to 'suck in' the sex toy and relaxing should feel as though you're pushing the device out of your body. Work up to ten repetitions a day. Once you've mastered that, treat yourself to a vaginal barbell or love balls, which you can leave in for hours at a time.

The longest-ever kiss took place in New York in 2005, and lasted 30 hours, 59 minutes and 27 seconds.

For him

It's an important muscle, but many men don't know where it is or how to locate it. The prostate gland and the urethra pass through the PC muscle, which runs from the tailbone up to where the penis attaches to the pubic bone. Because it connects the front, the back and all the bits inside, it stands to reason that if you strengthen the PC muscle, you can increase control and sensation in the entire genital area.

To locate your PC, stop and start the flow when you're peeing. Now tighten and draw in your anus as though you were trying not to fart, and hold your urethra as if you were trying not to urinate. Hold for three seconds and slowly release. Work up to 20 reps a day.

Supersize your sexercise. Because the PC muscles contracts around the prostate, having something up your butt can help strengthen the muscle and feel great at the same time. After a while, it'll help you last longer.

Sex is still the most popular search word on the internet.

Ann Summers

www.annsummers.com